MAPPING YOUR FUTURE

By

Mike Balof

© 2018, Mike Balof

I thank my son Bradley who edited my original course and gave me excellent guidance and counsel, Mom, Dan, who always encouraged me along with all who gave me encouragement and assistance in this endeavor.

This book is intended to support All who need help from within. It is not to be resold for profit. Up to 45 words of this book may be copied and used for editorial discussion or utilization in headers and banners on websites. Any other use including a larger than 45-word quote requires advanced permission in writing from the author.

Thank You to all those who aid in the needs of helping others everywhere.

You can also read this book online and make your notes in a notebook if you wish. The important thing is to read the book, and that you keep records of your ideas, to help you later.

© 2018, Mike Balof

WELCOME

AS WE START

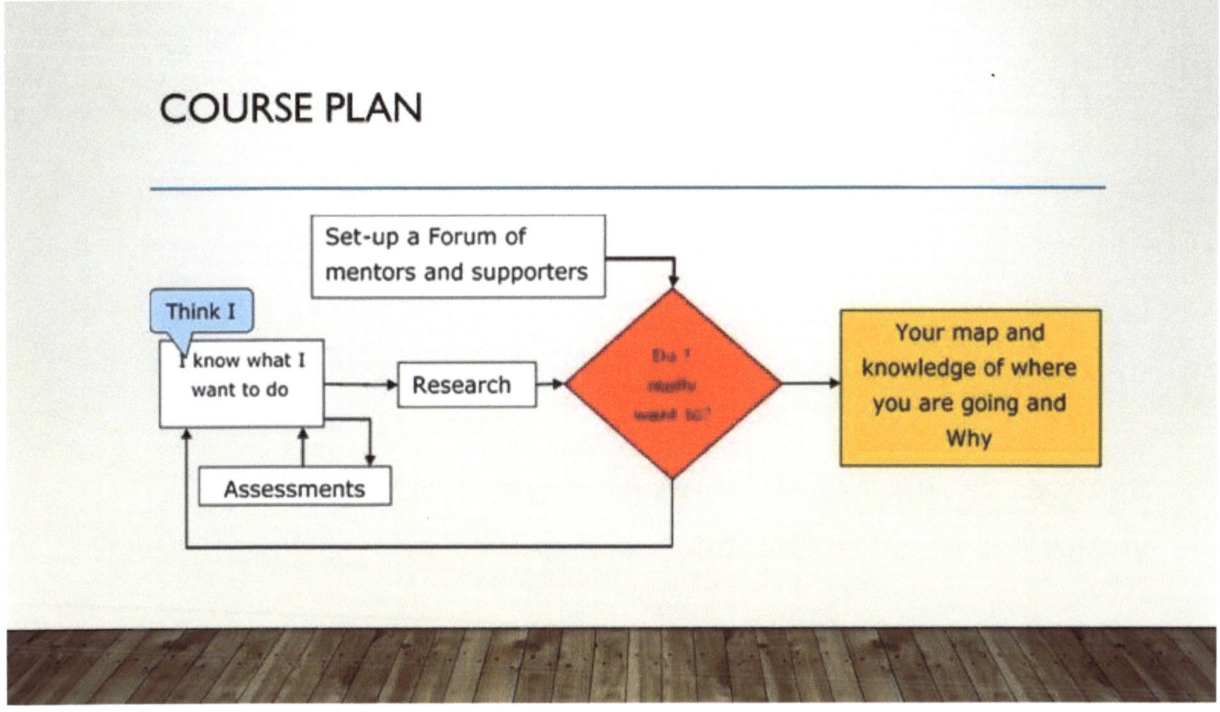

This book is a version of a book designed to accompany an E-course on mapping your future. If you wish, you are welcome to join my Reveille Facebook Group, ask questions and talk with others who have the book.

Please share this book with your spouse or significant other. If you are working on this book, and share it with your spouse or significant other, you have a better chance of success. Working together is important. It is also essential you do not force or coerce your spouse or significant other. They are welcome to take this course and should only do so of their own free will.

Please join our Facebook Group.

This group allows you to collaborate with your peers and share ideas and thoughts on the milestones and goals you are working on. You can get something done easier when there is a group working together.

Spouses or significant others are invited to be with you in our Reveille Facebook Group for free.

<u>Tangible Actionable Items</u>

Tangible action Items for this course include:

- Researching your next endeavors in life.

- Developing lists of who, what, when, and where.

- Deciding what you want to do.

- Understanding the milestones and goals to get to where you want to be.

- Developing a physical map of your milestones, goals, and objectives.

Not Planning Forsakes Goals

When you make your plans, and set up your timelines, start with who and what is most important to you. Then you must think and make plans for what it will take to sustain those people and things which are most important to you.

Make your plans synchronized to the movement of life. Those plans must meld with the time, the seasons, the phases of our lives, and our trek towards our goals and objectives. And while doing this, understanding that no matter how decisively we develop these plans and goals, nothing is guaranteed. At the same time realizing that not planning forsakes those goals to the whims and desires of everyone and everything else. Planning and goal setting is essential.

The first question is, "What do I want to be when I grow up?" If you're in high school, this is an excellent question. If you are in college, this is an even better question. If you're in your mid-20's and tired of service level jobs, this is a most needed question. In your 40's this is a mandatory question and believe it or not between 55 and 65 this is a vital question. These questions at each step of our life help to hone and know where we are and where we want to be. If you are not sure of your goals, how will you know when you get there?

For today, please think about what you would like to do in the future. At this point don't worry about money, education or other items. Think about what you want, what you think you would enjoy doing, and how that supports not only you but those people and things most important to you and write it down.

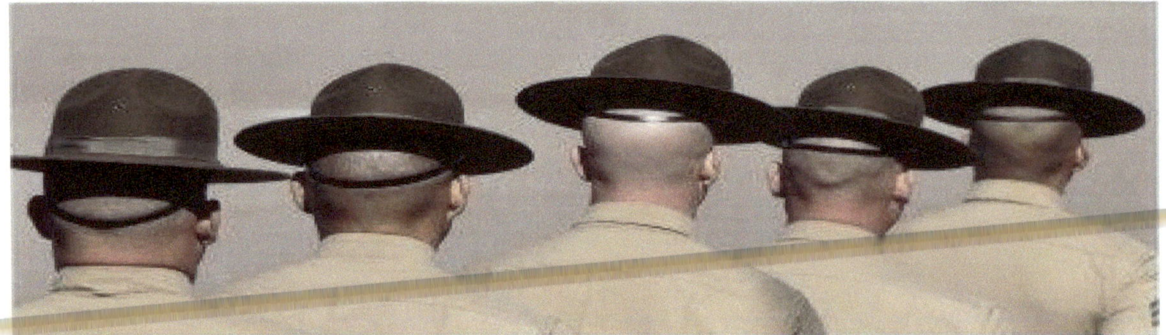

Ready to Accomplish Something?

Do you really want to improve the processes you use and reach your goals? The question and the answers are yours, and any solution is acceptable if it is your answer. Why is the statement true?

The only reasons and answers for what you do and strive for are yours. There are a thousand reasons why something cannot work, and some people are willing to give them to you. A reason to fail is only valid if you pick it up and use it.

With a thousand reasons to fail, you only need one reason to succeed. If you pick up and use the idea to accomplish something, it is more potent than all the reasons for failure. If you stick to your course, not let the 'Nay Sayers' beat you down, and keep your senses about you, you can accomplish just about anything.

Will changing your processes be easy?   Change takes work. Anything worth doing is worth working to accomplish. Just remember what Jim Rohn said:

"Discipline is the bridge between goals and accomplishments."

~Jim Rohn

What I Plan to Accomplish in This Course

<u>My and My Family Bio</u>

Where you have been, and where you are going in life.

As You Start the Book

As you start the book, you need to acknowledge that this is something you do voluntarily. You do this to better understand where You want to go, and what your best path is to get there. In this course, you are looking to find your goals, and the milestones it takes to get to those goals.

If you have a significant other, a spouse, and/or children, or anyone else you care about and will be taking along, it is good to ask them if they would like to take the workbook with you. Immediate families or significant others may do this for free. Please let this be a voluntary role for them and not something that is expected of them or they feel pushed into.

The Workbook will require planning, research, mapping for where you want to go in life, and finding the best way to get there. This course will also help you look at ways in which you can assure that your goals are the places you really wish to be in life. To do this, we will guide you in making the lists you will need, the websites that you've been to, and what knowledge you need to obtain along the way.

During the book, if you need extra areas for writing, feel free to print out an additional page or add a blank page from the workbook after the full page.

What Do You Want Out of Life?

Module One

We start with an inventory. This is a grouping of questions to help you establish a baseline you are starting from. There are no right or wrong answers. As long as they are your answers.

Define Your Goals

Look around you right now. What do you have that you like? Also, what do you have that you want to change? Please fill this out below or in your Mapping Your Future workbook on page 7.

____

____

____

____

No one ever really does it all alone.

Who do I have who helps me (mentors, supporters, Cheerleaders?)

Who do I have who helps me?

____

____

____

____

____

____

____

Those you take with you

Your will be who you are taking with you. Spouses or significant others, Kids, Parents or grandparents (or grandkids.) You may have Friends who may not be at a new location, yet still might be the ones you talk to and share things with. It is good to have them for morale and support.

Name	Relation	Remarks	email	Phone No.

What I want determines where I want to go, and how I want to get there.

What do I want from my life? Money? Fame? Happiness? Comfort? Friendship? Service to others? Paths' to greatness? Other?

Please fill this out below or in your Mapping Your Future book on page 9.

____

____

____

____

____

____

____

What am I willing to do to gain my goals and objectives? Can I do what it takes?

____

____

____

____

<u>Assessing the Situation</u>

Module 2

Now it's time for you to understand what your goal looks like. Be sure you're writing everything down and keeping track of who and what goes with you to your goal, and something new for you to keep an eye on, what and who do you pick up along the way.

The first step in knowing where you want to go is to see where you are right now. This is where the lists and notes you have been taking throughout this book come in handy.

You can be different and live in a cave and wear an old monk's robe and not do anything. You could also be a lottery winner. How often does that happen? Back to reality? OK.

What we need to help you find out is where you want to be, and then we want to work on how to get you there.

Remember, it does not matter how outrageous or costly or in need of education or any other impediment might stand in your way. This is just establishing what you would really like to do. The mere fact of writing it down sets you on the journey. It does not guarantee you anything. It is just a start.

If you are not sure, you can find a short quiz to take online. There are many free on the internet. The one I like, and which is free and given to you by the Department of Labor and the Department of Education is called my next move. The web link to it is www.mynextmove.org.

You can also check at local colleges, and other organizations in your area to see if the Myers-Briggs test is given anywhere near. The Myers-Briggs might be provided free by some organizations, and other organizations may want to charge a small fee to administer it. Look around and find your best bargain. Or, look for a free test online. Just be careful, some websites will offer you the test for free, and they want you to pay for results. I wouldn't do that if they did not tell you the cost up front. There are enough free sites out there.

Nearly free is a relative statement. I read a book on my Kindle that talked about $0.99 is the new free. I have also read articles about the internet making free the new free. I too have been suckered in on websites that offer a free assessment or computer checkup or something else for free, only to be told at the end that to find out the results or fix supposed problems I had to pay ($19.95 to $29.95 appears to be the going rate.)

I have adopted the philosophy of free is free until I am asked for the credit card number. Then, I click off of that site and look for another location. There are actually free sites on the web.

Assessments and information found:

www.mynextmove.org www.onetonlone.org https://www.careeronestop.org/explorecareers/assessments/selfassessments.aspx https://www.16personalities.com/free-personality-test

Good Information

www.onetonline.org

If you are not sure what you want to do, and you take some of these tests, they should point you in some pretty good directions. If you take the test, and you still are not sure of what you want to do, don't worry. Some of my best friends are over 39, and still trying to figure out what they want to do in life. They're good people, and I know that someday they will figure that out. Do the best you can with where you are and what you have.

One thing I should warn you about so that it doesn't happen to you as it has to so many people. Some people (and I have done this myself) don't figure out what they really want to do. They want to do everything. Rather than being happy with one goal and one direction, some people are always running around looking. Every time they hear something new from somebody, they are off trying it.

It's interesting to see new ways of doing things, and it's fun. It is also, some-times, very costly and leaves people empty. Why is that? Because they're looking in the wrong direction for the answer. Nobody knows you better than you do. Most of what's going to motivate you and make you work does not live in some webinar somewhere, it lives inside of you.

You are the person in control. You must live with whatever your decision brings. Paying others to tell you about ideas and doing everything for you is not very helpful.

It is good to take classes and learn things. When you pick something you want to be, do your research and make sure this is the path and the goal you truly want. A little research up front may save you from some real future mistake.

 Be sure to fill out the information and Question in Mapping Your Future book or below.

<u>Other assessments and Information sites I have found</u>

____

____

____

____

____

The big Question of this module.

What did you learn from the assessments?

____

____

____

____

____

____

Research

Module Three

Module one and two where a time of thinking and self-exploration while you looked at where you want to go in your next stage of life and what you want to do. Please remember, these answers might be understood with assessments, yet, the real desires come from you.

Module Three is Research. The more you research your desired goals in life, the better you will understand them and the easier it may be to obtain what you want out of life.

DOING RESEARCH IS CRITICAL

Trust, but verify.

Doing Research Is Critical

I learned this in basic training. This identifies why research is so important when you're looking at doing something.

When I was in basic training, in our second week we all went to a briefing and were given a chance to sign up for our jobs in the Air Force. I went into weather maintenance. It was a career field with a 9-month technical school. I learned all about electronics and the weather.

Others in my flight chose their desired profession. One of the airmen in my flight picked Fire Control Operations on a bomber. He was thrilled and very proud.

We asked him if he liked to fly. He said no, he did not want to fly. The obvious question then was why did he sign up to be a tail gunner on a bomber, with the Viet Nam War in high gear. He told us his position as Fire Control Operator entailed loading all the fire extinguishers and refilling them when and if the planes came back.

Everyone in the Training Flight tried to convince him otherwise, and he would have no part of it. Three days before the end of basic training the Drill Sergeant called the flight together. The drill sergeant told us about a hero-to-be in our midst.

The airman who volunteered to be a Fire Control Operator was being graduated from basic training three days early. The reason was the airman's new flight crew flew in to pick him up. They were waiting in a jeep out front, waiting to meet their new tail gunner.

It Actually Happened!

In this module, we will try to save you from an unwanted adventure. Please do research on your goals and destinations. Next, we will look at who to talk to, and about finding mentors.

Have you ever chosen to do something and then found out it really wasn't for you? What steps would you take to ensure you are not getting into something you really do not want to do?

Please write about this or on page 13 of your Mapping Your Future Book.

____

____

____

____

You need to do research and know what you are getting yourself into when considering what to pursue, especially if it is something that will be new to you. Here are some easy ways to do this.

Go to your browser, whether it is Google, Bing or some other and start by putting in a one or two-word subject about what you want to be. I would like to be a motivational writer so I will plug that into Google. Be careful of all the various places offering free items, and then wanting people to sign up for their paid services. My belief is free is free until someone asks for the credit card number. Then it is time to close out that search and go back to looking for the next sites to go to.

How do you know which websites are legitimate and which are not? I have a method that works well for me.

I will go to my browser, and type in the title of the company, or site, or organization, etc., I want to know about. I put two spaces after the title and then type in the word "scam." I am not saying the site I am checking out is a scam. I am looking to see if anyone who has posted to the web about the website, company, or entity being a scam. Real scams usually have a lot of returns to this kind of check. Here is another place where relativity comes into play. A large company no matter how good they are will have someone, somewhere complain about something. If only a few complaints show up, then you want to take note of them and keep them in the context of the overall picture.

For each position and company, you want to know the following: There are 5 of these pages in your Mapping Your Future workbook (also attached in the blog), and you can print extra sheets if needed.

1. What does the company do?

2. What do I like about the company and or the job?

3. What is there about the company or job that I do not like?

4. Do I have the skill sets to do the job?

5. Will this fit into me and my family's lifestyle?

6. Does the job pay what I need for my lifestyle? (Sometimes we need to perform lifestyle corrections for where we are at the moment.)

7. If the position is dull, dangerous or dirty, will it be overtaken by computers?

Add your own Questions to research:

8.

9.

10.

11.

12.

The Computers Aren't Coming, They Are Here

We have something new that you really need to consider when you're looking at goals. That new item is an old friend called technology. We all love technology.

Technology gives us wash-and-wear clothes that we can just throw in the dryer pull out and put on a hanger. Technology gives us everything from three-minute popcorn to being able to watch all the shows and movies for next to nothing without even having to leave the house.

 Computers allow us to talk to anyone in the world. To run our own business, and to do many other marvelous things such as the ability to look up anything we need to know at any time 24/7, and we can get a credible response.

Technology continues to grow exponentially today, it is now taking over jobs. We've all heard the talk about someday and some way. Well someday and some way, have arrived. There are 21 different jobs which automatons now do. An article in the Los Angeles Times reports that in the next 15 years 38% of work could be run by automatons. Thirty years out, it looks as though those numbers will more than double.

Look at the goals that you have set for yourself. Does anything include employment that may be considered dull and boring, dirty or filthy, dangerous or life-threatening? You may want to rethink careers that fall into these categories. The reason is those are the areas that are best suited for automatons to work in.

Humans will never be pushed entirely out of the picture. Yet the positions of humans who want careers done in mass by automatons will go to those who are outliers. That is to say, those who lead and innovate in that career field. You can be one of those if you are willing to do what it takes.

Supporters and Mentors

Module 4

Part of your research should be finding people who are willing to talk with you and give you some encouragement towards your goals. Trying to improve, can feel like trying to move mountains. Having people who are willing to help mentor you is a great benefit to your work and your morale. Find your supporters and invite them to be on your team as mentors, collaborators, partners or friends.

Most people are proud of what they do, and it is easy to get people who will talk with you for 20 minutes. It is easier if they can feel you are not going to put them on the spot, ask for a job, or take too much time from them. Below we have some do's and don'ts and some ideas for finding and setting up mentors.

Ask those who you admire and look up to in your profession if it would be all right for you to call them some time with a question. People who rise up in their business are frequently proud of what they do. Professionals like to talk with others about what they do and how it helps others. Most of them usually make time (20 minutes or so) to speak to someone or answer a few questions.

As the person seeking the advice of a professional or mentor, it is essential you not waste their time. When you talk with them, have questions ready to go. Pay attention to them. Ask follow-up questions; however, do not argue with them. Whatever you do, do not ask a professional who is giving you a little of their time for a job. Asking for a job would put them in an uncomfortable position and cause the interview to end prematurely. If they ask you, then you can give them a copy of your resume.

Exercise in Collaboration

Call ten supportive friends and ten people whom you respect and who work in the same profession you want to work in. Tell the friends what you are doing and ask if they could be part of your support group. Ask if you could speak to them, on occasion, about what you are doing.

Ask the professionals if you could ask them a question now and then and count them as a mentor. Keep track of who says yes. This looks hard, and you will be surprised how easy this exercise ends up being.

Please complete this exercise in the Map Your Future book, or you can fill out the chart here.

Call ten supportive friends and ten people whom you respect and who work in the same profession you want to work in. Tell the friends what you are doing and ask if they could be part of your support group. Ask if you could speak to them, on occasion, about what you are doing.

Ask the professionals if you could ask them a question now and then and count them as a mentor. Keep track of who says yes. This looks hard, and you will be surprised how easy this exercise ends up being.

Name	Position	Remarks	email	Phone No.

Many people will give you 20 minutes to ask a few questions about what they do and how their business actually works. If you ask to talk to anyone, they will probably say yes. When you meet with them, you want to ask real and specific questions and honor the time limit agreed to unless they wish to spend more time with you

Here are some Dos and Don'ts.

<u>Do</u>

1. Have questions ready.
    1. It is hard to think of the right questions on the spot.
2. Be polite, the person you are talking to is freely giving their time.
3. If you have questions based on what the professional says go ahead and ask them.
4. Be on time.
5. Dress professionally.

<u>Do Not</u>

1. Ask questions that you can find out from their (or their companies) Website.
    1. Do your research.
2. Ask them for a job.
    1. Asking for a job often puts them on the spot and ends the interview.
3. Waste their time.
4. Dress or act unprofessionally.

Here is a page you can use when talking with a professional.

What does a new person in an industry want to know about what they want
to become? Each of us will have different questions. Some of these issues
may be:

1. What does the professional I want to become actually do?

2. What are the pros profession I am going into? And, what are the cons?

3. What does the job I want to do pay?

4. What are the milestones in the business that I should look for to tell
   me I am doing well?

5. Who are the industry leaders in my profession and what sets them
   apart?

6. How much do the industry leaders make?

7. What is an industry leader's lifestyle in my desired profession like?

Other Questions You Have:

8.

9.

10.

11.

<u>Putting it all together</u>

Module 5

In this course, to date, we have talked and gathered information. I hope you found some good things and what you need to know. Our next step will be taking all that information and putting everything together. So let's go over a few things just to make sure that you have what you're going to need to map where it is you're going to.

Check through your booklet and any other notes you've taken to see if you have the following:

Yes	No	Question
		Have you decided who will be going with you on this journey? Spouse or significant other, friends, kids, extended family, pets, and possibly others?
		•Do you want to know what you want to do? Or what your overall goal is?
		•Do you have information from any assessments you have taken to help point you in a direction?
		•Do you have some supporters to give you encouragement along the way?
		•Do you have some mentors you can ask a question or two of from time to time?
		•Do you know what you need to get to your ultimate goal? What milestones must you map towards that goal?
		•Have you considered what the next steps will be after you reach your goal?

Please consider these questions and grab the information that you'll need from your notes and in the next chapter we're going to start talking about, and mapping where you would like to go in life and what you would want to do. Once you are ready and have what you need, please move on to the next module.

Finish Research and Start Map

Module 6

Did you get to do some research? Did you find what you wanted to know? If you are still doing research or trying to find something out, that is okay. The better the job you do with researching, the easier the rest of the process is.

Do you have Mentors and supporters now? Treat them well. They are better than gold.

Now it is time to plan your goals (where you want to be) and your milestones (the essential steps along the way to help you get to where you want to be.)

I think it is time to consider an imaginary trip.

If I told you to drive from where you are to the Great Salt Flats, and there would be a reward for you there, and you had no map or directions, and you could not use GPS or a computer, could you get there?

I would think you probably could. Though, the trip would be a lot slower and may have some wrong turns. It may take you a week or more for something that should only take a few days. There would be extra gas burned, and excess wear and tear on the car, and the people in the car.

When you get to the Salt Flats, you may find that you are 40 miles from a gas station. Also, there are no restaurants or hotels, freshwater or other places to fulfill your needs. You may have packed differently, or driven routes, or even took more provisions if you would've had a map and some facts about where you were going.

If you have decided what you want to do professionally, as a career, or the industry you want to work in, now is the time to start laying out the path of how you are going to get there. This is the rough overview. At this point, it is almost like saying, "I worked in the Air Force, and now I plan to be a process improvement developer." It is just a bare-bones, yet it is a start. Think of your goal and milestones as to the stopovers and destination on the road of life.

Milestones are important. We do not climb a staircase by jumping from one landing to the next. And, we do not get to go from start immediately to where we want to end up. If it is worth doing, you should do it well. Here is hat a map of getting to the Salt Flats and back, from a planning perspective might look like.

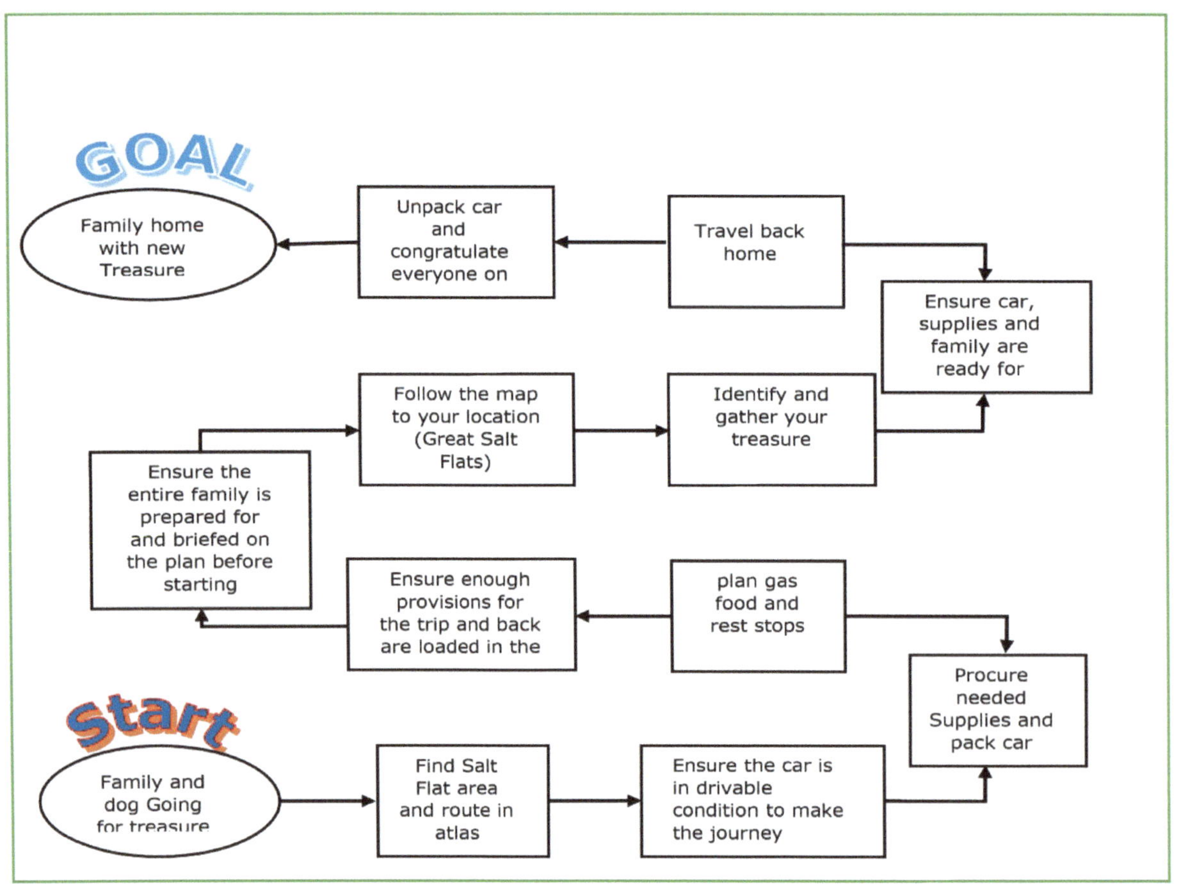

To help you with building your map of milestones and goals, I have made this template for you, I have put several in your Map Your Future Workbook.

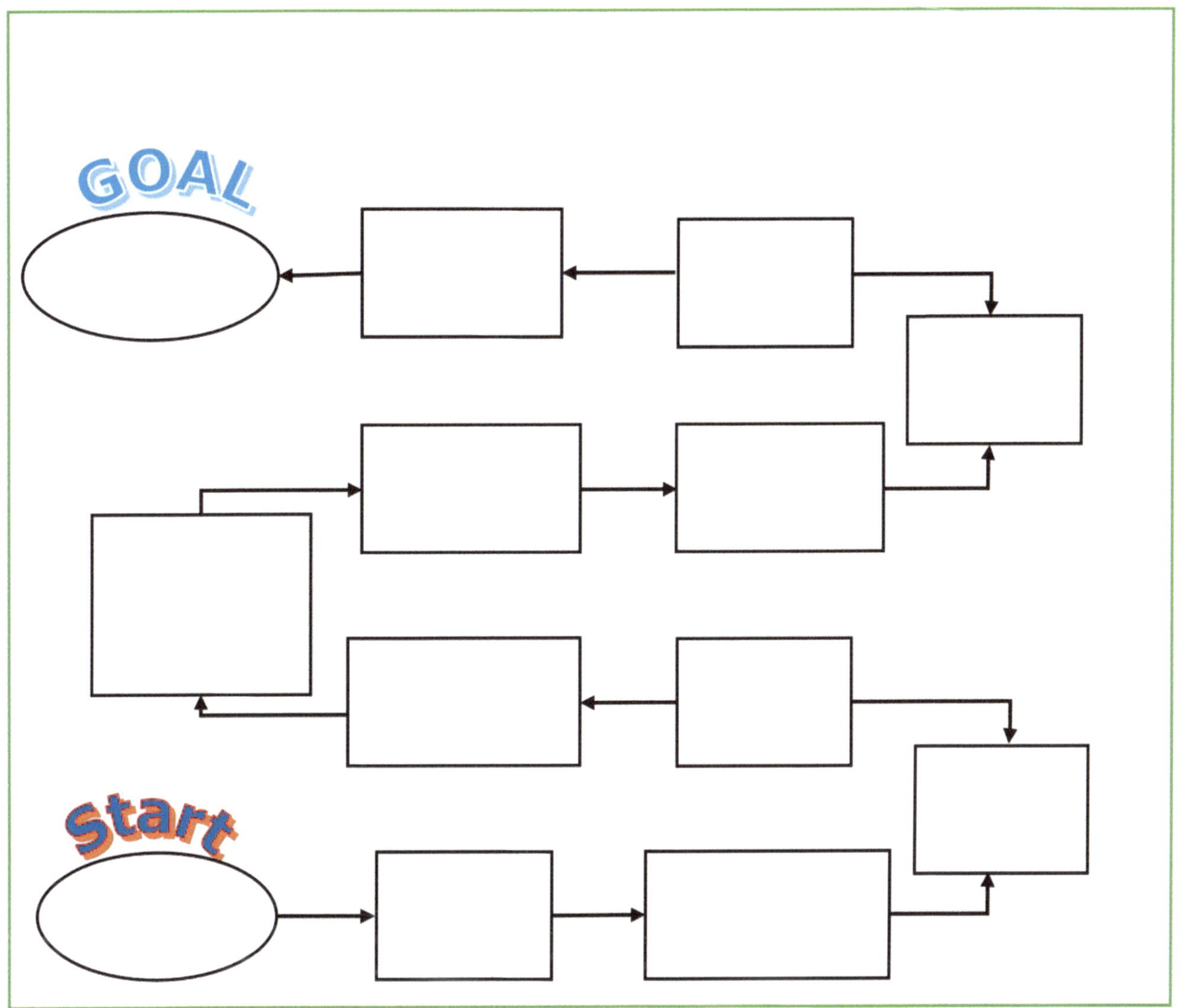

Your map will not be exactly like mine, I just wanted to offer a template. Each plan will be different because every person is different.

In this goals map, everything was made with icons and arrows, right from the insert ribbon on Word. The frame was added a little bit later.

We start where we are. On this map that is with someone living in a trailer and driving a motorcycle. As time goes on, we see a significant other is met, and a move to an apartment happens. The bike gets traded in for a sedan and as time goes on this couple makes a map of desired lifestyles.

The crib shows us that the couple will have a child. Then as time goes on, they will get their degrees. The apartment is given up for a house. Some work from home is started, which turns into corporate work. It looks like this job will give them what they want which is time to go play in the snow, do some skiing, and even win a few awards.

They learn a lot, keep on planning, and always take time to have some fun like going to a dance. They become leaders and speakers in their professions. And, finally get to the point in their life where they teach others, write books, run seminars and webinars to help others to do the same.

Your map may not look like this one either. Remember, everyone is unique,
and every map will also be unique.

Ideas

____

____

____

____

____

____

____

____

____

____

____

____

____

Here is another template you can use. Be sure to share your maps in the Facebook Group. You never know what kind of help and great suggestions you can get from others by sharing.

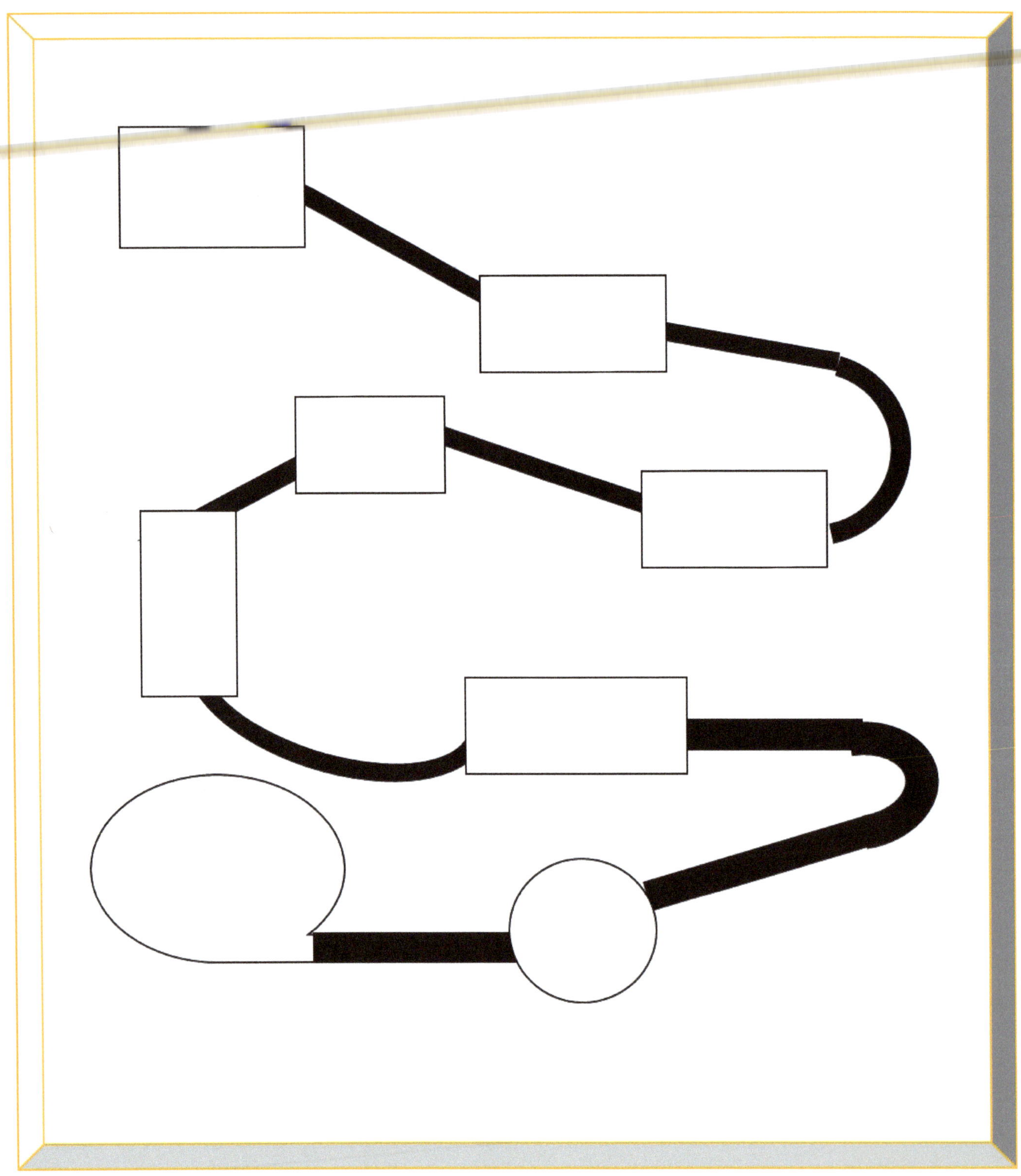

Beyond Goals

Module 7

I have a secret I'll share with you. The goal is excellent, yet it never compares to the fun you have and the people you work with along the way. Those are where the great memories are made. It is never the destination. It is always the journey.

Do you know what happened to the person who got everything desired? That person lived happily ever after.

~ rewrite from Willy Wonka

If you have technical problems with your map, please send me an Email, and I will help you with it. mikeb@reveille.rocks. I know that a life transition can be a really rough time. The goal here is to relax and plan the future together with those who care about you

Summary

We've gone over quite a bit in this course, and I thought it would be good to take a moment and recap a little bit and help anybody who has any questions.

We started by stating what we wanted to be or what we wanted to do. If not sure, some assessments would help us figure out what our interests are or what we might like to do.

After that, we started to research what was involved in becoming a professional in the area we were looking to work. We asked a slew of questions. We also found some supporters and mentors, to make sure we knew what we were getting into.

Next came a reality check. With all the recent knowledge found, are we sure we want the life and work that we sought at the beginning of the process? If not, research into a different line of work should have been initiated.

Finally, we mapped the path and the milestones we needed to follow to be successful in our new profession (our Goal.) The map is a visual reminder of what we would like to do and where we would want to go.

When reaching your goal, you may find it to be more a part of the journey and not an end. That is when you want to map your next goals and milestones. Use this course if you like and write to me. I would be glad to help.

You are Almost Done!

Congratulations on your hard-earned progress in this book. Thank you for reading it, and I hope it will be of use to you.

Before you go, I wanted to share some extra resources that you can take advantage of right now to continue your learning:

- www.onetonlone.org - Developed by the department of labor, you can take free assessments and find out about any job or career you are interested in pursuing.

- https://www.careeronestop.org/explorecareers/assessments/selfassessments.aspx - learn more about jobs

- My next move: an excellent assessment to give you an idea of what you would like to do.

www.mynextmove.org

- AARP: The link below will take you to page on people who changed jobs or started a second job after fifty.

https://www.aarp.org/work/career-change/info-2018/great-secondcareers.html

- Please remember I have a free course which you are welcome to enroll. It is 'Always Employable.' If you have any questions after you go, please don't hesitate to send an email or talk to me in the Reveille Facebook Group, or you can messenger me, or you can email me at mikeb@reveille.com.